IT HAD TO HAPPEN

Written by

Kretena Monek Hunter

"Pain Birthed My Purpose"

© 2021 by Kretena Monek Hunter. All rights reserved.

Published by Pamela D. Smith

Printed in the United States of America

ISBN: 978-1-7377896-2-8 (e-book)

ISBN: 978-1-7377896-3-5 (print)

No part of this book may be reproduced in any written, electronic, recording, or photocopying without the written permission of the publisher or author. The exception would be in the case of brief quotations embodied in the critical articles or reviews and pages where permission is specifically granted by the publisher or author.

All scripture quotations are taken from the NIV and NLT versions of The Holy Bible.

Acknowledgements

My Father, Jesus Christ for the discipline, wisdom, understanding and courage to birth this book.

To Lawyer Heath Hattaway, never stop doing what God called you to do. You're Awesome! Thank you for everything.

To my precious children Deontrell, Malek, Amyani, and Alexis. I love you. May you find hope and the courage never to give up.

To my precious grandchildren Heaven, Malachai, Haisley, and Kade. I love you. All of you are the reason I strive to be better everyday.

To my sisters April, Amanda, and Latoya- thanks for all the love and support.

To my lovely mother Gracie, thanks for your love and support.

To my encourager and prayer partner, Katriva Straughter- thanks for always listening and being a phone call away.

To my Aunt Betsy, thanks for always being by my side and supporting me.

To my late Aunts, Hattie Sue Henderson Simmons, and Barbara Ann Shine Gunn, whom I miss very much. Both of their deaths have helped me to grow in ways I never imagined.

And to you who hold this book right now, the hurting heart, the disappointed soul, I know your pain. I really do. I also know God sees and hears you. God loves you no matter what. My prayer is that the burdens you're holding on to, are lifted off you as you embrace the truths through the pages of this book.

Table of Contents

Introduction 1

Chapter 1: The Perfect Love Story 4

Chapter 2: The Storm 11

Chapter 3: The Shipwreck 19

Chapter 4: Faith Walk 26

Chapter 5: God's Peace 34

Chapter 6: The Exoneration 41

Chapter 7: Completion 47

About the Author 52

Introduction

Life is like an endless book; everyone has a story, and its chapters are limitless. Like books, life teaches us many lessons about sorrow, difficulties, and pain, which often have a stronger impact on us when compared to the lessons of happiness, pleasure, and prosperity.

Love is a never-ending desire of human beings. We all want someone to truly love us. The flame of love always burns inside our hearts because love is an attribute of our Lord. He created us with love and care as His children and kept that love in our hearts. He sent us on the earth with our soulmates, so all we need is to find the right one. Whenever you find true love, it's always a blessing of God, His sign of care; therefore, He sends someone into our lives to care for us on the earth.

"The best and most beautiful things in this world cannot be seen or even heard but must be felt with the heart."

~Helen Keller~

But what if that person is not sent by God? What if he was sent by the Devil instead? A son of the Devil who can destroy your life entirely. Someone who erases the smile from your face and fills your life with all darkness and dullness, who puts your life at stake for his/her benefit.

That is exactly what happened to me. A person came into my life and changed it completely. I thought he was a blessing from

God but, in fact, he was a curse. He tried to absolutely destroy my life by snatching my pride and honor. What I thought was true love came into my life and I trusted him blindly, but he tried to ruin me.

This is my shocking story, the journey of my life that moved from a fairyland to hell. In **March 2017**, my life utterly changed. I was in lockup for a felony I never committed. I was charged with multiple counts of money laundering, theft, and conspiracy with a five-million-dollar bond. How did I get there? The story must be told!

Amid constant lies with no truth in sight, I still gave my life a chance. That's the way America works, right? Everyone deserves a second chance. So, my friends, co-workers, family, and people in the community, I'm here to ask for mine.

I am a loving mother of four kids with a bright future ahead. And I am giving you a chance to walk in my shoes by detailing what it is like to deal with a controlling narcissist. I'm not searching for sorrow. I am just presenting my side of the story to you. It was the most painful experience of my life after which I was unable to trust anyone again except God. God has always been with me in my life through thick and thin. So, in this horrible nightmare, I kept on trusting Him and He brought me out from the darkness. This is a story of my firm belief in God. This is also a faith book about how God has had grace and mercy on me because of the calling I have on my life to teach and witness the gospel to everyone.

We all are his amicable creation. He loves us more than anything and wants the best for us. But there are always two powers in the cosmos God and the Devil. You must decide who you will trust. If you choose God, then get ready to be tested. He tests our beliefs in our bad times and if we stay connected to Him, He brings us out of all difficulties. This was my test and I successfully passed it but not before enduring excruciating pain.

As you read this book, I pray you will recognize the importance of being vigilant and you should never trust anyone blindly. Check on the person's background and those of their families, friends, and other associates. That angel you think you know could be the Devil dressed in white with a halo. The person could be a wolf in sheep's clothing waiting to tear you apart for his/her own benefit.

"Never give up, for that is just the place and time that the tide will turn." ~Harriet Beecher Stowe~

CHAPTER 1

The Perfect Love Story

Love is an undeniable fact of our lives. Everyone wants to love someone and be loved in return. Love fills our lives with colours, hope, happiness, and beautiful emotions just like a blessing from God. When God is happy for us, He sends His blessings in the shape of love to us. So, whenever you find true love, it's always a blessing from God. It is His sign of care. He sends someone into our lives to care for us on the earth. But it's not always true in every case. There are exceptions. And the challenge is often identifying the difference.

Sometimes love comes into our lives, but we cannot retain it. Circumstances, situations, and the phases we pass through make it tough to handle and hard to continue. People give up on love or get bitter after encountering bad situations. The situation I faced made me vulnerable and devastatingly broken due to my divorce. I considered it the toughest time of my life because I was having issues with my husband, but I was not expecting it to turn into a toxic relationship. I ended up being mentally and physically abused. This was the most painful time of my life, and I was suffering from mental unrest. I usually had arguments and fights with my husband over different issues. Maybe it was an age gap that caused us not to understand each other. My husband was three years younger than me, and we were infinitely different from each other.

In harsh situations, we need someone to give us comfort, even if only temporarily, especially when you feel insecure and lack trust.

We were both betraying each other. Due to mental unrest, I was looking for a corner to hide and a shoulder to lean on, someone to give me hope, even momentarily.

We are not perfect. We make mistakes, sometimes lots of them. The key is to learn and move on. They become our lessons. The error I made being disloyal to my husband was a lesson for me. I got pregnant, and I thought the baby was my husband's. But later, I discovered she belonged to another man I had slept with out of hurt. This was the last nail in the coffin of my marriage. In 2010, we got divorced.

A broken pregnant woman with her other three children was fighting for her survival all alone. But I took a stand to fight back.

I considered myself the transgressor and limited God. I was plagued with guilt and felt bad about it all. I remained connected to God throughout that period and eventually, He healed me. He healed my broken heart with hope and forgiveness. I was being restored to a life I was ready to accept once again. My baby came into the world, and she filled me with hope, love, and the joys of motherhood. Life was again on track and things were getting normal by the grace of Jesus.

I believe in forgiving others because God always forgives me.

"Be kind and compassionate to one another, forgiving each other, just as in Christ God forgave you."
Ephesians 4:32, NIV

I am a strong believer in God. He always enlightens my path by forgiving me and showing me the way. He also taught me the lesson of forgiving others and moving on. Therefore, I forgave myself and my ex-husband for everything, and I was ready to move further.

"Bear with each other and forgive one another if any of you has a grievance against someone. Forgive as the Lord forgave you."

Colossians 3:13, NIV

I started nursing school classes again. But my life was about to change again, and I had no idea. After such a tough life, I thought things were going to be all right. I was focused on my career and wanted to take it seriously because it was my last hope of revival financially and mentally.

Things were normal and I was busy at my job but there was always a lack. I wanted someone to understand my pain, what I was going through and how lonely I was. I wanted to give myself a second chance. But my emotions and feelings were not for everyone. I wanted someone special who would touch my heart deeply with uncontrollable passion. Such desires are not in our control, and we cannot overcome these feelings when they knock at the doors of our hearts. You are simply consumed by the person for whom your heart pumps. Something similar would happen to me. Someone was relentlessly knocking at the door of my heart.

It was Mr. Newbie who was going to completely turn my life around. I met him on a college campus. He was a grad student majoring in Criminal Justice, and I was a nursing student in the process of transitioning from an LPN to RN, where we were both attending school.

Some people have strong personalities that attract us at the spur of the moment, especially when you are a sapiosexual. I am always attracted to people with strong personalities and amazing intellectual senses. He was a killing combination of both attributes.

He had goals of becoming a lawyer and knew how to speak and when to speak. His personality was charming and would impress anyone. In a very short time, we got very close and became good friends. Love starts from friendship. Being with Mr. Newbie always gave me a positive feeling of hope that God was sending happiness into my life.

Eventually, Mr. Newbie signalled his love by sending me flowers, gifts, and cards. Well, this was the first day, when he asked me to go on a date. I was aware of the feelings he had for me because I felt the same for him. I was drowning in love and ready to believe in his everything. What does a broken and lonely lady feel when she is bearing all the pain alone and doing double duty at school and home?

She desires sheer attention, as well as someone who cares and makes her feel special like never.

He called me superwoman just because of how I was surviving. He was very aware of that. Honestly, I was starting to smile again and wanted to try this dating thing. This man quickly gained my trust and that of my family. I was going through my healing process and really wasn't ready to date just yet, but he was very persistent.

I did not receive that much attention from a man in years, so yes, I was smiling from ear to ear. Truth be told, I was still holding on to hurt from my marriage and hurt people hurt people. But how long could I resist his charm?

What does a woman want from her partner? Is it a lavish lifestyle, out-of-town dates, and dinner? No, sheer attention and care, a charming and intellectual personality to mesmerize her, as well as a good house and a financially stable person who is willing to share all her pain and make her happy. He was a complete man with a charming personality. In front of him, I was vulnerable and could not restrain myself from his charm. I did not want to make any decision so early, but I was susceptible to him. I was feeling happy, and everything was moving quickly. I spent almost a year with him, and my family and I trusted him. Everything was going perfectly.

Key Take-Aways

- Love is a blessing.
- We are not perfect. We all make mistakes. The key is to learn and move on.
- Deep inside we all have an inherent desire for love and affection.
- God loves and heals us despite our transgressions.
- Forgiveness is important if we want peace.

Make It Personal

"Bear with each other and forgive one another if any of you has a grievance against someone. Forgive as the Lord forgave you" (Colossians 3:13, NIV).

Why is it important to forgive?

_____
_____
_____
_____
_____
_____
_____
_____

Is there someone in your life you need to forgive? Why are you finding it difficult to do so?

_____
_____
_____
_____
_____
_____
_____
_____

Why should you forgive someone who has hurt and betrayed you?

To-Do List

1. Make a conscious effort not to speak negatively about those who hurt you.
2. Meditate on Colossians 3:13 and Ephesians 4:2.
3. Start journaling your thoughts.

Prayer

Father, thank You for the blessing of love that brings bright colours, joy, and happiness into our lives. Thank You for showing the greatest love of all when You sent Your Son to die for us. Lord, as beautiful as love is, sometimes it ends in hurt and abandonment. I feel the pain. My heart is broken. Heal me, Father, and I shall be healed completely. Take away all bitterness from my life due to past relationships. Help me to forgive those who hurt me as You have forgiven me. Open my heart to love again. In Jesus' name. Amen.

CHAPTER 2

The Storm

As a famous proverb says, "life is not a bed of roses." Instead, life is an everyday test. You must pass through that test and be revived again. I had already spent almost two years of happiness. However, a massive tornado was headed my way. I was getting some storm warnings, but I was not prepared for such major mental damage.

During those two years of my life, Mr. Newbie changed a lot but still, I remained with him. I thought I might be wrong about him. Perhaps I was overreacting and should give our relationship a chance until and unless God reveals something big to me. That's what I thought. He was not the same person I perceived him to be in the beginning. He was turning into a controlling narcissist. He started to track the contacts on my phone and wanted to reduce my social circle. He just wanted to take control of my life and my children's lives. I really don't know why he changed his attitude, but I was praying for God to reveal his reality to me. At least, I wanted a sign to tell me if he was the right person for me or not. But that was only a trailer; the real thrill was about to start in my life.

On **December 30, 2015**, Mr. Newbie was arrested and charged for motor vehicle fraud in Hudson. This news was as shocking to me as any other person. I was dating him for two years but never knew what was really going on in his life because he was a very private person. I was also okay with that. I accepted it as his nature, a part of his personality. For me, keeping personal space was not an excessively big issue. But what God revealed in front of me was shocking. In fact, it was incredible.

But that mess was not for Mr. Newbie alone; it was waiting for me as well. After Mr. Newbie's arrest, law enforcement came to my job harassing me. Apparently, they were investigating me but, in fact, they were humiliating me for being a Black woman. They just wanted to show me as a bad Black nurse. I told them what I knew but for the most part, I let them know Mr. Newbie was a very private person and didn't let anyone into his personal space. Of course, they didn't believe me.

In this place, Blacks have always been discriminated against. This was not the first time I was facing discrimination based on my color. It's the story of every Black person. But I always have faith that my Father, our God, is with me. I knew I was not alone. God would heal and bless me and drag me out of every hard time.

They had already entered my home and ransacked it. They put my two daughters who were minors to stand outside in the cold without any adult present, but who could stop them, especially when they were not ready to listen to a single word I had to say? My kids were suffering out there in the cold. At this time, I was a nervous wreck and wasn't thinking about my rights until I spoke to my cousin who practices law in the state of Texas. After talking to him, I was a bit more confident. I was about to fight for my survival.

The state police came back to my home on **January 6, 2016.** They were trying to question me some more and record me. However, I refused to talk to them anymore without an attorney present. They continuously threatened to arrest me. I was humiliated by their behavior. I told them repeatedly I knew nothing about Mr. Newbie's fraudulent activities, and I was not associated with him, but still, they were trying to fit me into the frame as an offender.

On January 8, 2016, the state police came to my job and arrested me. All of this was very embarrassing and a military tactic to see if I knew anything, but honestly, I didn't. People are married for 20 years or more and have no clue what their partners are doing. We didn't live together, and I worked all the time. I had no time to keep up with his business. I was taken to jail and made a bond in an hour.

My God was with me as He says,

"The Lord himself will fight for you. Just stay calm." Exodus 14:14, NLT

I was fired from my job and my name was scandalized all over. Everywhere I applied for a job I was turned down. No one would hire me due to this matter. The financial stress was insurmountable. I had to take care of my family and I was out of a job. I became depressed but despite that, I kept praying, fasting, and applying for jobs. My connection and trust in God never left.

I was exhausted and cried profusely. I felt as if I was going through an arid desert where wild creatures were ready to attack me. Sometimes, I felt as if I was just roving and roving, hoping, and praying to find an oasis but there was nothing in sight. Nevertheless, giving up was not an option!

> "There is no failure except in no longer trying." Elbert Hubbard

So, I continuously tried and at last, I was hired at a job 30 miles from my hometown. A long-distance job but still that was a hope. At my interview, I was totally honest about everything and was hired on the spot! I knew it was God just showing me He was in control. Man can say no but when God says yes, nobody can change that. So, again, it was God's indication, He is with me. All I needed to do was be patient and have faith. As my Lord says:

> "Do not be afraid or discouraged, for the Lord will personally go ahead of you. He will be with you; he will neither fail you nor abandon you." Deuteronomy 31:8, NLT

One month later, my former employers called me back and said after careful consideration and investigation, they were wrong to fire me. I was innocent until proven guilty and I could have my job back if I wanted it. So, I went back to my job with my head high but still ashamed. However, God covered it all up. I continued to fight to get my life back, and I was trying to recover from the shame and embarrassment. I was embarrassed to face everyone to whom I was connected. I stopped talking with people because all they did was blather and gossip about me. I could feel the smirks and stultification in their behavior. Social isolation is a curse. People you were accustom socializing with suddenly change. Your colleagues, friends, and sometimes relatives turn into strangers when you pass through hard times.

I continued to pray and serve God at my church while back and forth to court fighting charges of the theft of motor vehicles because they were parked in my yard. This was a very trying time for my family and me, especially my children because they were getting picked on at school. I was away from my kids and worried about them. The state was trying to portray me as a careless mother who was involved in crime and unable to teach and train her children as a good person. This pain made me pray harder and prayer made me powerful.

"Pain doesn't just show up in our lives for no reason, it's a sign that something needs to change."

Author Unknown

Key Take-Aways

- Life is an everyday test. You must pass through that test and be revived again.
- Don't ignore your intuition when it is talking to you.
- Opening yourself to someone takes courage and trust. It can be risky.
- Stay calm. God will fight for you.
- When God says yes, no one can change it.
- Pain is a sign you need to make changes in your life.
- False accusations are enough to destroy a person.

Life Application

"Do not be afraid or discouraged, for the Lord will personally go ahead of you. He will be with you; he will neither fail you nor abandon you" (Deuteronomy 31:8, NLT).

What are you struggling with right now?

Are you holding on to something or someone you know deep inside you need to let go of? Why? Why not?

How will letting go make your life better?

_____
_____
_____
_____
_____
_____
_____
_____

Read Isaiah 43:2-5. What does God say about your hardships and difficult times?

_____
_____
_____
_____
_____
_____
_____
_____

To-Do List

1. Write down in your journal how you feel today.
2. Write down two things you want to change about your life.
3. Write down how you can make those changes.
4. Visualize your future when those changes are made.

Prayer

Father, I have been hurt and betrayed by the person I love. False accusations have been made against me. My friends and family have deserted me. But You will never forsake me, you will never leave me. Though all the world forsakes me and Satan plots evil against me, you will fight for me. You will plead my case. You will make my enemies my footstool. And when all is said and done, I will overcome. In Jesus' name. Amen.

CHAPTER 3

The Shipwreck

A new beginning is always hard, especially after experiencing mental trauma. That was my case after getting out of jail on bond. I was gathering all my energy to start my life. It was a hard time for me because it seemed as if it was a cycle where I broke up, got healed, and was ready for survival again. We all make mistakes in life. Mine came with a heavy price: peace and rest. Yes, my peace and rest were compromised due to all these things.

I never imagined anything like this could happen to me. I can still remember the night I went home from jail. I was in a state of shock. Although I managed to get released on bond in one hour, I was traumatized by the severity and enormity of what had transpired. Everything was playing out like a movie in front of me. The demons of my past were chasing me, and the menace of the present was making me restless. The phase of happiness was very short in my life.

I thought about my mom and dad. It is true when we suffer from pain, we always remember our parents. I love my dad, but I could not stay with him for a long time. He moved to Dallas when I was a baby, so I only saw him on holidays and occasionally, in the summer. He wasn't really involved in my life at all, but I love him a lot. I was often searching for him through relationships because I had this vision of how a man was supposed to be. I know my father is a very successful and intelligent man. I always wanted a man like him, but the truth is I think they were just the opposite. None of them were whom they betrayed to be.

A real man listens to a woman, is polite, stays with her, instead of abandoning and betraying her. A real man understands a woman and forgives her for the mistakes she has made, just as our Father in heaven forgives us. A real man is honest and protects a woman instead of deceiving her and trapping her in false charges of theft.

Every single thought was pounding like a hammer in my mind, and I was desperately trying to run away from them. After my family, the faces of my friends and co-workers were smirking in front of me. They were trying to show me how evil I was, that I was a thief, not a kind, caring, and hard-working nurse, who was laboring day and night to earn legitimate bread for her family. We do not think about our words, how harsh they could be, and how deeply they can hurt others. In the hurricane of all these thoughts and emotions, I didn't remember when I got asleep.

The next day was a little bit refreshing because I was with my Aunt Ann. She was motivating me to be strong, telling me it was not my fault, that whatever happened to me is in the past and everything would work out in the future. I was not the type of person to give up. I was a fighter and would fight to the end. I was broken like a ship and had to pick up the pieces and start again. I was trying to keep my life on the right path but that was not so easy. Nevertheless, God was keeping me. God was motivating me that everything would be alright, and He is with me. I was becoming more and more obedient to God, and I was strictly following His path.

I was working as a nurse, had changed my number, and no longer had any contact with Mr. Newbie because God showed me so much about him that I didn't know. In 2017, I said I had to be obedient to God. Mr. Newbie tried to convince me everything was a lie, but God revealed it all. The Devil knows God has a plan for my life. He was trying to do everything in His power to stop it. He knows I am a blessed child of the King, and he was trying to bring every obstacle in the way of my faith.

In March 2017, once again, the police showed up and arrested me on the job. I remind you they had my address and knew my work schedule. But once again, it was a tactic to embarrass and humiliate me, as well as make me lose my job. That way, I would not have the resources to fight for myself. Oh, this time, they surpassed themselves and hit me with money laundering, conspiracy, and theft charges. All I could say was, "God, you are in control and the thieves only come to loaded vaults." This time, with these charges, my bond was five million dollars. My family and I did not have that kind of money and they knew it. Of course, I had to sit in jail until my court date to ask for a bond reduction.

I believe whatever happens in your life is for a purpose, I stayed in jail for 31 days but while I was there, God used me to witness to other women. I helped several people to get to know God and give their lives to Christ as well. Teaching about God is a holy task, and I had to exercise my faith in Him. I held Bible studies and prayer sessions three times daily and just kept reading. It had to happen.

After 31 days in jail, I went to court. My lawyer fought hard that day to get me the bond reduction. There were so many emotions in that courtroom as the prosecution tried to paint a picture of me as a threat to my community. Can you imagine? They were arguing that because of theft charges, I was a threat to the community. But they were openly discriminating against me just for being Black. I was helpless in front of them, but all my hopes were in God. I trusted Him to bring me out. People discriminate but God never does.

The judge granted the bond reduction to $100,000 but I was short $12,000, so I left the courtroom crying and hurt because I was going back to jail. I said, "God, you are in control and whatever you are trying to teach me, my ears and eyes are open." God replied to me through the verses of the Holy Bible:

> *"For I know the plans I have for you,' says the Lord. 'They are plans for good and not for disaster, to give you a future and a hope."*
>
> *Jeremiah 29:11, NLT*

I said, "God, only You can fix this." Little did I know God had my two sisters/friends working to get me out at that time. Later that night around 9 p.m., the guard called my name and said, "Get your stuff, you made bond!" I had just finished a Jericho walk, and I screamed, "Lord, I thank You," with tears dripping down my face. As an innocent woman with a career and my entire life at stake, this was very devastating, but tears of joy were flowing. These were the tears of faith that I have in God, and He maintained that trust and faith by gifting me my freedom.

God replied: "Fear not, for I am with you; be not dismayed, for I am your God; I will strengthen you, I will help you, I will uphold you with my righteous right hand."

Key Take-Aways

- Starting over is difficult, especially when you have been mentally traumatized.
- Watch your words. They can heal or kill.
- The Devil comes to steal, kill, and destroy.
- God can use you even in your darkest hour.
- People discriminate but God does not.
- When we surrender to God, He will take over.
- God's goodness and mercy will always exceed our thoughts.

Making It Personal

How are you responding to God in your times of trouble? Do you have a clinched fist (anger) or open hands (trust and surrender)?

What can you learn from Hannah's response to pain and struggles in 1 Samuel 1:1-18? What was the outcome?

_____
_____
_____
_____
_____
_____
_____

What can you learn from the author's response to pain and suffering? What was the outcome in this chapter?

_____
_____
_____
_____
_____
_____
_____

What does Jeremiah 29:11 say about God's plans for you?

_____
_____
_____
_____
_____
_____
_____

To-Do List

1. Finish these sentences after reading the scripture verses in brackets.
2. It is God who------------------------(Jeremiah 29:11).
3. It is God who------------------------(Deuteronomy 31:8).
4. It is God who------------------------(Psalm 73:26)

Prayer

Dear Father, thank You for making a plan for my life. Thank You for being a personal God, for being involved in the affairs of my life. I know you love justice, and You will vindicate all who put their trust in You. Lord, I surrender my life and all its conflicts to You. I know you are in control, even when it does not look that way. Help me to follow Your ways. You know best. In Jesus name. Amen.

CHAPTER 4

Faith Walk

Revival is always a hard process but after talking to God through signs and verses of the Holy Bible I was being revived. I was aware all my difficulties would come to an end, and I would have a normal life. I had absolute faith in God, and I was ready to start once again.

Released from jail and searching for work, I was trying to pick my life back up.

After meeting all my financial obligations, I was preparing to see my daughters. I was ready to bring them home once again. It was the first time I had seen them after a month. I could not wait to see them. I love them so much. Doing those thirty-one days in jail without my kids was heart-breaking for me. I was worried about how they were living without me. I missed them a lot. I wanted to go back home to kiss and hug them. If you are a parent, you can understand this deep pain, especially if you are a mother whose children are your world.

It was all my fault. I felt guilty because I trusted Mr. Newbie so blindly. How could I have done that? Why didn't I do any background checks? Why didn't I get more information about him and his family? As I pondered on these thoughts, I felt like a big failure. I had failed as a parent and was not a good mother. The mother inside me was crying, shattered, badly broken, and burdened. All my efforts to succeed in life were going to zero.

Heavy-heartedly, I had to face the music. I had to go with the flow. I had to feel this pain because it was all my fault to trust someone as a blessing of God when, in fact, he was a real lesson.

We usually ignore some things when we are emotionally attached to someone. We only look at the attractiveness of that person and ignore the fine details. But that one mistake of mine turned my life into a living hell.

I was already in a vulnerable situation after what happened in my marriage from 2002 to 2010. That was a long time to spend with someone. Couples fight and have issues, but they resolve them through dialogue; however, we decided to divorce after separating several times. When I met Mr. Newbie, he was like medicine for my hurting soul but what I thought would cure me, became poison to my life.

My children and I were separated for a while, but my friend helped us get back together. He stood by me in my darkest days, through thick and thin. He liked me but he was not the one for whom my heart pumped, so I never considered him seriously. He did me a great favor being there for my children when I could not be. Everything in my life was happening with the help of God. He never comes to the earth Himself, but He sends his holy messengers and people to help us. He helps us in ways we do not expect.

"God never gives up on us. You may think of all the reasons why you can't overcome, why that problem is too big, and how it's unbearable, but God is going to keep calling you a mighty hero." ~Joel Osteen~

The news of my arrest was a hot topic for the media. They were framing me as a thief and money launderer. I was released on bond for these big charges, but it was spicy news and a hot topic for the media to discuss. They wanted to promote the lies to society that this Black woman was involved in crime, how bad and evil Black people are, and all the crimes in society originate from us. Due to this news and my arrest, the nursing board was about to cancel my license. My last way of fighting back was about to end. I had already paid every cent I had to get bail and now I was about to be stripped of my livelihood if my license got suspended. I was worried about my children because the state would take them away if I was unable to meet their needs.

But I was still hopeful because my God was still there and when He speaks, everyone becomes silent. When He decides to bring you out, nobody in the world can keep you behind bars. When He stands with you and holds you up, nobody can make you fall.

I wrote the nursing board to plead my case, so my license wouldn't be suspended. They were not ready for this. But due to my continuous efforts and communication with them and after providing them with all the material details about my case, the nursing board did not suspend my license. After over a month of searching, I was finally given a chance at PPNH, thanks to great references. I have always been a hard-working, caring nurse, performing my duties with great care and caution because I love my work. Therefore, due to my true dedication to my work, I was appointed as a nurse at PPNH.

God was still showing me He was with me, His daughter. He said He would never leave or forsake me. I'm blessed God never took His hands off me. I know everything was working in my favor because I was obedient. Having faith in God and being submissive to Him is the real success of life. When we modify our choices according to God's, He loves us a hundred times more and gives us the best. When you feel alone and abandoned and have no one to help you in the entire world, I encourage you to pick up your head and don't give up because God has not left you.

> *"The steadfast love of the LORD never ceases; his mercies never come to an end; they are new every morning; great is your faithfulness"*
>
> Lamentations 3:22, NLT

God is waiting for you to give all your burdens to Him. He takes all our pain and gives us rest when we are obedient. When we love Him, He loves us back and takes all our pains and sorrows just as Jesus did for us. He bore the agony and pain for us and became a path between light and darkness. He took the pain for our salvation and sacrificed Himself. This is the lesson we should learn. We must be ready to make sacrifices. God tests our love and when we are successful in showing love for Him, He does wonders. Sometimes we try to fix situations ourselves when all we must do is give it to God and He will work it out.

Don't let FEAR (False-Evidence-Appearing-Real) paralyze you and keep you from reaching your destiny. Every day I went through this, I never knew what the outcome was going to be, but I trusted God. Whenever you feel stricken with pain, think about this: the knife must be sharpened by striking and rubbing it against something strong before it can become useful. You will be great after the struggles. We all face tough times, but we must be faithful and strong enough to fight back.

However, you will not succeed with a head full of negativity and overthinking. If negativity blocks your thoughts, how can you hope for a positive outcome? Without positivity, there is no way out. Believe me; there are only two ways: light and darkness. The light always comes through the darkness. Light becomes more visible in the dark. You will have a lot of things to consider that are negative but few that are positive. But you must focus on the positive. I tried to find every possible way out of my darkness and was continuously praying for God to show me the lightened path.

I continued to block out the negative thoughts and replaced them with positive ones. Someone said to me one day, "If I had walked in your shoes, I probably would have given up and lost my mind." I replied, "With God on my side, I will not fall, and I rebuke anything the enemy thinks he has in store for me."

When you find yourself stressed out, beaten down, on the verge of giving up, remember God is with you, and He understands. Find the strength to trust God, no matter what it looks or feels like. Nothing can separate us from His love.

"Neither death nor life, neither angels nor demons, neither the present nor the future, nor any powers, neither height nor

depth, nor anything else in all creation, will be able to separate us from the love of God that is in Christ Jesus our Lord."

Romans 8:38-39, NLT

Key Take-Aways

- Revival is always a difficult process, but it is possible.
- Admitting our mistakes takes us one step closer to healing.
- A good friend sticks closer than a brother.
- God takes our pain and gives us rest when we are obedient.
- Replace fear with faith and negative thoughts with positive thoughts to succeed.

Make It Personal

Do you have a healthy perspective on the circumstances in your life? Why or why not?

_____
_____
_____
_____
_____
_____
_____
_____

Identify your regrets. What do you constantly blame yourself for?

Read the following verses. What do they say about regret?

Romans 8:1

Matthew 11:28

Philippians 3:13

Hebrews 8:12

To-Do-List

Say these affirmations out loud daily

- God does not condemn me.
- I will forget the past and look ahead.
- God does not remember my sins.
- All things are working out for my good.

Prayer

Father, thank You for Your steadfast love that never ceases. Thank You for Your mercies that never end. They are new every morning; great is Your faithfulness, O Lord. Men may remember my sins and mistakes, but I will not remember sins You have forgotten. My hope and trust are in You. Lord, help me to block out negative thoughts and overthinking that will stop me from overcoming any obstacles. In Jesus' name. Amen

CHAPTER 5

God's Peace

Peace is priceless. Your mental peace is yours and you cannot let anyone play with it and turn it into unrest. I would say we should keep ourselves calm and peaceful and try to control our emotions. For example, a bottle of water in comparison to a soda, when you shake a bottle of water, it stays calm and peaceful. However, when you shake a bottle of soda it fizzes and bubbles. We ought to be like the water and not the soda; otherwise, all our emotions will erupt by even the smallest shaking. On the other hand, if we are like the water, we will be calm and consistently peaceful. When you become over-emotional and show your weaknesses to everyone, those weaknesses can be used against you. If you are calm, you can think more positively and approach situations with greater caution.

Protect Your Peace; It Only belongs to You and God

Nobody can love you more than yourself, so how can you allow someone to hurt you and steal your peace? Let others know to approach you with caution! They have no right to disturb your peace. Protect it at all costs. Everyone doesn't deserve a place in your mind and heart. Love the ones who genuinely love you but remember you must love yourself first. I've discovered that my peace and energy are all I can control on my own, and I'm entirely responsible for securing them. I had to look at the things I had around me and make some changes if I wanted to prevent being depressed and frustrated all the time. It's a challenging journey to preserve your peace and it will not be easy. But once you get serious about the things that are influencing you negatively and take some action to correct them, you will begin to feel better.

Your peace is yours to preserve. Do not let your heart be shaken by anything in the world. Make sure that, regardless of all the external influences, you have contentment. Maintaining your peace puts everything else into perspective, encourages you to hold your peace and walk with a smile on your face throughout the day.

Chances are something will happen that keeps you a little on the edge, but 90% of the time, by just being mindful of what drives your actions, you can have a better emotional day. You are opening space to use your energy and have a positive effect on the world around you. It's an attitude that says I'm trusting God, and it speaks volumes to people. It takes time, focus, and the grace of God to be consistently peaceful. Most of the time, our stress levels are tied up in our circumstances. You can be stressed for many reasons but it's up to you if you stay in that place.

To conquer the stress in our lives, we must learn to practice the peace Christ Jesus gives. I learned to develop peace by living in the now and thanking God for right now, the present.

Each time He said, "My grace is all you need. My power works best in weakness." So now I am glad to boast about my weaknesses, so that the power of Christ can work through me." 2 Corinthians 12:9, NLT.

We can spend a lot of time thinking about the past or wondering what the future holds, but we can't accomplish anything unless our minds are focused on today.

Trust the Process; You Will Figure It Out!

It can be confusing and hard at times. This is where there is a lesson for you to learn or an opportunity to grow. Trust that you are meant to be here, and better days are coming because God is here for you, and He will do everything in his timing. One day, He will heal your broken heart with His love and care; He will give you peace and abundance. But you need to trust His process. You are having exactly the experiences you need to elevate you to your next level. Keep faith that everything will be alright. Everything takes time to be settled. There is no magic wand that will change the situation, but the process will bring change for you. Trust the process of God.

The Bible tells us God's grace is sufficient, and it works best in weakness. I believe God's grace is the power that enables us to do what we need to do. It's not what happens to you; it's how you respond to it.

"That's why I take pleasure in my weaknesses, and in the insults, hardships, persecutions, and troubles that I suffer for Christ. For when I am weak, then I am strong."

2 Corinthians 12:10, NLT

We need to stay strong amid all our hardships. In your toughest times, stay strong and trust God because He alone can change your situation. Staying strong does not mean you have no emotions. Rather, it is the ability to express your emotions and press on. Staying strong is, "I'm feeling this, and it hurts. I'm going to let myself feel it, cry, and talk about it, then I'm going to move forward." Moving forward is the rule of life, and it's always painful. It's painful to move with all your memories whether good or bad. The burden of the memories could be heavy to carry with you, but you cannot run from them. The more you run the more they chase you. All you need is to stand strong and face the pain by trusting that God shares your pain. It might be difficult, but eventually, it will make you much stronger.

Face the pain and stay strong. It isn't about showing the world you never feel anything other than happiness and confidence. Staying strong is being brave enough to admit you do, but though you are hurting, you are moving forward anyway. Staying strong is pulling yourself up out of the darkness and moving forward with faith that your God is with you.

I always believe everything will be alright, even when it doesn't seem like it. This belief kept me alive, even in jail. My time in jail was extremely hard because I really did not know what would happen to me. I had no idea how long I would stay in that jail. I did not know if I would get out or not. These thoughts nagged me daily, but I believed my God was with me, and He would make my situation better. He would not abandon me and leave me there alone. My faith in Him kept me fighting. Even though I was going through so much and felt defeated, somewhere deep inside, I knew eventually, everything would work itself out, even when it didn't seem that way. This belief inspired me and gave me the strength to fight despite the hardships in my life. I was determined to survive in every circumstance.

No matter what it looks like, feels like, or what the past was like, I always trust God to bring better days for me. I knew my heart would not always be heavy when I awaken in the mornings, because God will turn my hardships into ease and would give me mental strength and peace.

Challenging days are a part of our lives and test for us; they guarantee better days are coming. Stay positive and calm, although it is the most difficult thing when you are fighting several issues, including finances and emotions. However, positivity brings good things. I believe in the theory of relativity. If you pray for good and declare good things, ultimately, they come to you. It all depends upon the intensity of the wish you want in your life.

When I was fighting in my darkest times, it was my Lord who was with me. It was His love and affection that saved me from being broken and shattered. It was God who repaired my thousand times injured soul by His grace, love, attention, and kindness.

The Lord talks to us in the Holy Bible:

> *"Be strong and courageous. Do not be afraid or terrified because of them, for the LORD your God goes with you; he will never leave you nor forsake you."*
>
> *Deuteronomy 31:6, NIV*

And that is what He did with me when I strongly decided to follow His path after being in darkness. It is all by His grace. I am content and thankful for everything I have and all the lessons I have been taught.

Key Take-Aways

- Your peace is yours to preserve. Do not let your heart be shaken by anything in the world.
- Develop peace by living in the now and thanking God for the present.
- You are meant to be here, and better days are coming.
- In your darkest hour, God will fight for you.

Make It Personal

Do you think you can have peace? Why or why not?

Where does the Bible say peace comes from? Read John 16:33; 2 Thessalonians 3:16; John 14:27.

To-Do-List

1. Set aside time to be alone with God (take a walk; listen to gospel music; pray)
2. Live in the present.
3. List five positive things in your life.
4. List five positive things about your character.

Prayer

Heavenly Father, you are the God of peace. You promised to keep me in perfect peace when my mind is fixed on You. No matter how much trouble is in my life, peace is possible. Teach me to focus on the positive qualities in my life and how to live in the present. I know hardships will come but You will give me mental, emotional, and spiritual strength to conquer. I receive all your promises for my life. In Jesus' name. Amen.

CHAPTER 6

The Exoneration

After almost four years of fighting charges and back and forth to court, all charges were dismissed. I was exonerated. The tears of joy filled my eyes. The feeling of being cleared was incredible. I could not believe they had acquitted me. But I must believe it because it was not, they who did so; it was my God, my Father who did this for me. I was confident He would bring better days for me, and finally, the day came when all my beliefs were turning into truth. I cried and praised God thanking Him for it all after my lawyer called me and gave me the awesome news. I knew this day would come; I just didn't know when. This is what faith is all about—things you can't see. I was taught patience through this waiting period. Discipline doesn't feel good while you are enduring it, but the reward you will reap afterward will be worth it. God stayed with me my entire life, even in the darkest moments. He talked to me as He says:

"Because of the LORD's great love, we are not consumed, for his compassions never fail. They are new every morning; great is your faithfulness."

Lamentations 3:22-23, *NIV*

To All My Black Girls

My advice to Black girls everywhere: whenever you find yourself in a room where there aren't a lot of people who look like you --- be it a classroom, or a boardroom, or a courtroom ---- remember that you have an entire community in that room with you, all of us cheering you on.

~Kamala Harris, VP

At that time, I still had unanswered questions like why the media didn't go back and tell the public I was innocent just as they scandalized my name when they thought I was guilty. This world is materialistic. We consider financial losses as the main deprivation but, in fact, the actual loss is emotional, for which you cannot be compensated. I was exonerated, but would the court be able to compensate me for all the emotional loss and distress I endured due to false charges made against me merely on suspicion? Would the media be able to bring back my pride and honour that was smashed by their fake news? Would my colleagues and friends who abandoned me in my time of trouble be able to face me when they were proven wrong? These were all the questions perplexing my mind and giving me a mixed feelings of joy and depression. Suddenly, a small voice whispered to me:

> *"And when you stand praying, if you hold anything against anyone, forgive them, so that your Father in heaven may forgive you your sins."*
>
> Mark 11:25, NIV

> *"But if you do not forgive others their sins, your Father will not forgive your sins."*
>
> Matthew 6:15, NIV

These were the verses of the Bible, which came into my mind as an answer because God always forgives us. Forgiveness is an attribute of God, as God forgave me, I forgave them all for whatever they did to me.

All is well, and I learned to thank God in every situation no matter what. It had to happen for God to prepare me for where He was taking me. Life was about to go on the right path. My job was going well. I was ready to get back into school to finish my RN degree. My friend was with me and this time, I was considering him seriously to start a relationship. I believe we should value the emotions of others, especially of a person who stands with you in your hardest times and is ready to accept you with all your good and bad qualities.

I was happy, content, and full of joy. This was also a message from God to me:

"Always be joyful." 1 Thessalonians 5:16, NLT

"Never stop praying." 1 Thessalonians 5:17, NLT

"Be thankful in all circumstances, for this is God's will for you who belong to Christ Jesus."

1 Thessalonians 5: 18, NLT

That's what I was doing in my life. I enjoyed it with my family and loved it. Once again, I was active in my social circles with my friends. I was performing my duties at home and work with full dedication. I was on the right path with God and regularly praying and fasting. I was thankful to God for everything and for dragging me out from what I had faced in the past.

"Even in dark times, we not only dream, but we also do. We not only see what has been, we see what can be. We shoot for the moon, and then we plant our flag on it. We are bold, fearless, and ambitious. We are undaunted in our belief that we shall overcome; that we will rise up."

-Kamala Harris, VP

Finally, I was in a self-created heaven and enjoyed my home as a garden of Eden. Life was complete but still, something was missing like a piece of the puzzle, which if put in the right place would complete the picture. I was broken and needed a shoulder to lean on. My friend with whom I was starting a relationship was that shoulder, but as you know, feelings come from the heart, and you cannot bring them forcefully. Also, after my husband and the incident with Mr. Newbie, I was not able to trust anyone. I thought all men were the same. I believed they were all cheaters and would eventually betray me—although I had pardoned both. Trust was not easy for me. I thought my friend would also betray me and ultimately, leave me with more hardships and heartbreak. So, I started to take him for granted and paid little attention to him.

"We all make mistakes, have struggles, and even regret things in our past. But you are not your mistakes, you are not your struggles, and you are here now with the power to shape your day and your future." Steve Maraboli

---

"Be alert and of sober mind. Your enemy the devil prowls around like a roaring lion looking for someone to devour."

1 Peter 5:8, NIV

Key Take-Aways

- Emotional losses can do greater damage to our lives than financial losses.
- Discipline doesn't feel good while you are enduring it, but the reward will be worth it.
- God uses troubles and trials to take us to our destinies and fulfil our purposes.

Make It Personal

What are some things you can expect in this imperfect world? Read Psalm 41:9; Proverbs 14:22; Psalm 109:22.

_____
_____
_____
_____
_____
_____
_____
_____

What does God promise you in your times of trouble? Read Psalm 9:9; Isaiah 49:15

To-Do-List

1. Create a gratitude journal.
2. Spend time in prayer and fasting.
3. Exercise
4. Bless someone unexpectantly

Prayer

Father, I know with You I will overcome. No weapon formed against me will prosper and every tongue that rises against me will be condemned. Lord, you will vindicate me. I do not need to fear or worry because You will give me the victory. When men fail to give me justice, you will take up my cause and deliver me. Thank You, precious Father. Amen

CHAPTER 7

Completion

I was always told the number seven means completion. I was starting life over as a free woman with all charges dismissed, while Mr. Newbie was convicted and serving time in jail. I never met Mr. Newbie again, but I forgave him for everything he did to me because I believe forgiveness is the path of God. When we forgive others then God forgives us. Although, I was disappointed with Mr. Newbie for everything and all the lies he told me, I prayed for God to show him the right path and enlighten his heart.

I started dating someone, and I admit I was not healed, but I was in the healing process.

When we are in the process of healing, we want someone to be there for us, to collect our broken pieces and turn us into the person we were. I was in the hustle of repairing my broken heart but still in search of someone to mend my brokenness and fill my life with happiness.

"And we know that God causes everything to work together for the good of those who love God and are called according to his purpose for them."

Romans 8:28, NLT

Being human, I deserve a chance—a chance to stay happy, a chance to find someone who loves me with equal sincerity, a chance to find a person who could share all my sorrow and grief.

Hurt People, Hurt People Once Again

I got engaged to that person but deep in my heart, I knew this was not the one. The number eight continues to stand out and I am always told it means new beginnings. I was compromising and continuously snubbing the voice of my heart. I knew he was not the one I was looking for but still, I was with him to heal my broken heart. I remember the day I took off my engagement ring to call off the relationship and went to return it to him—but I couldn't do that.

On January 8, 2020, I was arrested again because of this man who was supposed to have loved me and I was engaged to. I was about to get married to him but what can I say about a wolf dressed in sheep's clothing? Yes, he was a wolf who was dressed nicely and looking for someone to be his ladder, so he could achieve his ulterior motives.

I asked God how I made this mistake again. God said, "You are human, and it had to happen." God immediately whispered to me, "If I did it once, I will do it again, daughter. Just be still because I did this to save your life." That first rodeo was preparation for this one.

To Be Continued…

"You intended to harm me, but God intended it all for good. He brought me to this position so I could save the lives of many people."

Genesis 50:20, NLT

Key Take-Aways

- Forgiveness is the path of God. When we forgive others then God forgives us.
- We all desire to be happy and find sincere love.
- Sometimes God places us in difficult positions to save our lives.

Make It Personal

God has a great plan and purpose for your life. He is in control. Describe what the following scriptures say about God's sovereignty: 1 Chronicles 29:11-14; Nehemiah 9:6; Proverbs 21:1.

_____
_____
_____
_____
_____
_____
_____
_____

Given what is written in the preceding scriptures, will you trust God to take care of you? Why or why not.

What does Scripture say about God's protection over you? Read 1 Chronicles 29:11-14; Nehemiah 9:6; Proverbs 21:1.

To-Do-List

- In this list, I share with you some of the activities I do that help me tremendously in my life. I recommend you try these and watch your life change for the better.

- Make a prayer wall and every day, write out prayers on note cards of different colors. Go back and read them, especially when you need a reminder God is in control.
- Journal daily and write your thoughts.
- I send out daily devotions and prayers to over 100 people every day. You do not have to do this, but you can reach out and find other ways to encourage people even when you're going through difficult times.
- Pray. I do a 5 a.m. prayer call when God leads me to do it. Be obedient when God calls you to do something.

Prayer

Dear Father,

I know you love me with an everlasting love. Help me to surrender to Your control knowing You have set a hedge of protection around me to shield me from the works of the Enemy. Satan has come to steal and destroy my life, but You will give me victory over him and his cohorts. Father, I know I will overcome. I will arise and fulfil my destiny. I will conquer the lies, betrayal, discrimination, and afflictions because You are fighting for me. All the fiery darts of the enemy will be quenched. In Jesus' name. Amen.

About the Author

Kretena Monek Hunter is a nurse, author, entrepreneur, and encourager for Christ. She was born and raised in a small town in Louisiana. Kretena is passionate about helping others, especially broken women. Her passion was birthed through her own brokenness.

Kretena went through her Jonah experience, where she wrestled with God and ran from her purpose. She went through many difficulties that she knew was due to her disobedience. This initiated the beginning of her radical obedience and birthing of her ministry. Kretena encourages others by sending daily devotions to over 100 women and men daily. She serves as a board member for a Non-Profit Organization that helps young women build character for the future. She has been an introspective person who loves reading and journaling to express her feelings. Kretena is the oldest of her siblings, Chasity and Tanekquer. She has four children and four grandchildren who motivates her to become a better person daily. She strongly believes that Jesus came so that we could learn how to live out our Jeremiah 29:11 lives in abundance. Kretena wants you to acknowledge "It Had To Happen" in order for God to birth the purpose he has for you.

Journal

....
....
....
....
....
....
....
....
....
....
....
....
....
....
....
....
....
....
....
....
....
....
....
....
....

Journal

Journal

Journal

Journal

Journal

Journal

Journal

Journal

Journal

Journal

Journal

Journal

Journal

When life hits you hard, always remember don't give up! We fall, but we get back up again. We all will have troubles and hardships in this world. Always remember it's not what you go through; it's your attitude while you go through that determines your altitude. There is always a testimony after the test. Sometimes we cause some of our own hardships, but even when we do, God still forgives us of all our sins. Those who overcome great challenges will be changed and often in unexpected ways. Our struggles enter our lives as unwelcome guests, but they bring valuable gifts. Once the pain subsides, the gifts remain. These gifts are life's true treasures, bought at a great price, but cannot be acquired in any other way. After reading this book, my prayer is that you accept "It Had To Happen" and learn from it by moving forward.

Blessings,

Kretena Monek Hunter

"If you must look back, do so forgivingly. If you must look forward, do so prayerfully, However, the wisest thing you can do is be present in the present. Gratefully."

-Maya Angelou-

www.ingramcontent.com/pod-product-compliance
Lightning Source LLC
Chambersburg PA
CBHW062154100526
44589CB00014B/1827